The Gate at Visby

Poems by Deena Linett

for Richard
with every good wish
and peace.
Deena
March '12

The Gate at Visby

Poems by
Deena Linett

Tiger Bark Press ✦ Rochester, NY ✦ 2011

Published by Tiger Bark Press,
202 Mildorf St., Rochester, NY 14609.

Book design by Philip Memmer.

ISBN 13: 978-0-9816752-5-1

For Lev

May you *savor the indigestible grit of the world*

&

for George Petty

who does

Contents

I

II

III

The Prose Middle

IV

V

I

Earthsong

A woman in the temperate zone falls asleep
in early spring and wakes when leaves
are falling, days wrapped in somber tapestries.
Her presence adds one slender thread,
strands sparkle pink or mauve. Light
comes and goes, and the seasons.
Always it depends on where you are.
Earth tilts and turns and we–
    –why should we be spared the dark?

Scientists score thinking, lay strands
of neural impulses on staves and play–
brass and woodwinds, pitch of voice
and *clack* of sticks, eleven million twinklings.
Life leaps and lurches, quivers, pauses:
each little shock yields music.

Time torques. Light behaves as it will,
passing through gravity fields (no cows,
no green or flowers). What grows there's bent,
deflected. In wind and sun and rain
each day the Earth sings C#
as it turns, its songs like ours inaudible.

Each in Her Sacred Separateness

Mary pushes her hair off her face
at an outdoor pub in Rose Street,
Edinburgh. Crowds of passersby
drunk and happy, feathered, painted,
dyed and dressed for Festival, greet
their mates with shouts, embraces.
Her gesture is so natural and private
it seems a small note briefly struck
on summer in a little wind. For a time
it doesn't matter that she, like me,
has brought three living children
from between her legs. Just now
she's free, immaculate of touch, completed.

Invocation and Confession to the Earth Gods in Winter

Sir and Mother. There were a million
million moments, occasionally
one sharp enough to penetrate confusion.
The skies were more beautiful than we deserved
and though we loved them purely night
would come. We sacrificed grain and berries
that our children would live but some
did not flourish and we were not able
to save them. Please forgive us
for thinking these bright blooms
we took to ourselves were freely chosen.
We know now: we were mere rings in trees,
the serum of life a stream burning
through heartwood using us for its own purposes.

Child-Bearing

The girl who never breathed. Slip
of my first son between my legs,
his brother's hand trailing my thigh. Her head.

I can't see the sex. I ask. *A girl,*
they say, as if it happens every day
and hold her up before me, living
bluish flesh, first breath.

It takes ten minutes for the sun
to clear the horizon, twenty minutes
in bed with a good man, thirty minutes
to bring my only living daughter out.

Gratitude runs like milk.

June 6

My daughter and I leave Dublin
in a fine mist with the Sunday *Times*

and a loaf of bread sweet as cake
and heavy with raisins. This day

marks thirty-five years
since I said yes, I would marry

her father. Yeasty scent
fills the car on our drive west

to Galway over narrow roads
hung with flowers, past cattle

who don't care if we're Catholic
or Protestant. She's shown me

the harbor at Howth, dark stones
gray-green as ocean, the monument:

May we be gathered in the nets of God.
She drives. We sing. Talk rides

like foam on porter. Impossible
to have imagined this girl, this

day. It was Cambridge, Mass,
probably sticky. I was not yet

twenty-one and had managed
not to imagine tragedy. It must have been

an act of will. In 1944 the war
turned on events this day and I

would have been born in London
had my grandparents stayed.

I might have lived, dust
from falling buildings in my porridge

or died there, without this child
this day, gray alien anniversary,

the days as full as war
of passion, fury, and surprise.

Stalheim

Wind bends spiky wild grasses.
Midsummer fifty years after the war

following a tour-guide's gesture I climb
down steps into a World War II bunker:

Norwegian sentries here watched out for Germans.
Inside the wide stone vault, curved cool

goldwhite chamber lit by sun from somewhere
I look through a fist-sized hole in the stone

onto the entire miles-wide valley: *Twelve blues,*
Norwegians say. Rocky outcrops, stunted birch

and maple. Spruce stunned by wind,
brown tangled scrub all the way to the river

at the bottom of the Stalheimskleiven,
deepest gorge in Europe. A Jew

in peacetime I remembered icy nights
in moonlight. No one could see me.

The Man with the Sword

We want to know how he can do it
we want him to suffer, we want
his limbs to fail, his hands. We want him soft
and weeping.

Whether he's shaken, in the hours before, by dread,
whether he prickles and sweats, whether afterward
he dreams dead sheep and children, beats his wife,
silent through everything. She dare not utter,
speak or sing. In childbirth alone she can't be silenced.

Lost in Leaves and God

He taught me names of all the trees
we saw from windows on deep woods
in Lowland Scotland through a dark June rain.

I imagine George in a Trabzon orchard,
in the desert, on his *haj*. I imagine his wife,
young and beautiful, jet hair covered,

eyes cast down. Probably I'm wrong. Probably
her book-bag rhymes with a long easy stride
in tee-shirt, denim skirt, and sandals.

We lose people or they choose to be lost.
Months ago I gazed at openings of caves
near tops of rocky golden hillsides

near Masada and the Dead Sea, waved
at guards high in their watch-towers
across the fabled Jordan–all that land

without trees, burnings sands where history
remains to shape the daily. This icy night
on the edge of the Great Plains beside the Wabash,

my spirit reaches for the endless world,
deserts and forests, faultlines and volcanoes.
I want to see lichens' smatterings of color

on their local stone, yaks browsing, carpets
laid on sand, tents hung with bells, and imagine
George in Saudi, where it's not quite dawn.

for George Messo, whose poem
"In a Trabzon Orchard" gives
this poem its title

Souk, Akko

As roads in all the world are torqued and bent
by the terrain and habits of the living
the souk descends from markets under scanty trees,
shelter from the desert, cool and windless
and enclosed. Stone-lined avenues meander west,
drawn toward the inland sea, or east to Mecca.
Heaps of apricots and dates on trays
of hammered copper, woven cotton draped
from lines and folded, complex patterns
and geometries like antiphon to the abayah.
Scent lifts from piles of oranges and figs,
pomegranates, dates, bananas. Flourishes
of local stone stud silver ornament
and hand-worked gold. Sharp as circumflex
a turn before the mosque's façade: stones wet
with the day's scrubbing, and narrow streets
beyond choked here and there by bales of hay,
sacks of pistachios, arrays of fresh-caught fish.
Time's harmonics tremble in the souk's dry air
gathering the living, traces of the sacred
and profane, and in the wake, shapes:
oxbows and arabesques, wide and slow and flexed.

Khan al Umdan, Akko

Disused rest-stop on trade routes,
crossroads, caravanserai, the empty khan

feels still a place of gathering—as if stores
of spices, figs and barley, dates, pistachios

and apricots remain laid up in the interiors,
camel trains waiting in a splash of dark

beneath a few exhausted palms, and men
drawn together smoking, buying, selling,

telling news from travels through Egypt, Syria,
Sudan. One has silk cloth all the way from China,

another sacks of cinnamon, vanilla. Arcades
of stone stacked up along two floors

line all four sides around the sandy square
and its dry fountain, the whole an invert

Palace at 4 AM in floods of sunllight.
Between the arches, cadences of light and dark

like a periodic sentence, like heartbeat,
choruses, recurrences in stories, and verticals

reprise like longing, that most human tone.
Reversal and refrain— *open closed yes no*

light shade now later now never.
Carved above the single door-sized entry

emblems of Ottoman sultans, and a clock
that looks to the present in Jerusalem and back

to Istanbul. Seven thousand years
of habitation and incursion: Phoenicians

and Egyptians, Romans and Crusaders, Turks.
Now a Muslim town in Israel, no women

at the harborside but me, American Jew
on a bench a dozen steps from the souk.

The call to prayer inscribes blue air and no one stops
to listen—or to pray. Small boys chase a puppy,

older boys ride mules and horses to the wharf
where boats haul in the long day's catch.

Nets full of silver echo light-dashed water
bright against the old boats' rusted rigging.

Small waves lap the seawall where a cart
beneath a bright umbrella sells soda and kebabs.

For the Pinakothek der Moderne in Munich, William Forsythe, an American who lives in Germany, will make an installation piece "that takes the form of a blizzard of paper pieces bearing the names of dead Iraqi civilians in Arabic. As the tiny papers rain down, visitors will be forced to make a choice: to flick them off or allow them to settle on their own bodies, thus making them performers in the piece."

–NY Times, Sunday, February 18, 2007, 33 Arts.

N
ARABIC
M
PAPER
S(MALL)

NAMES
R
PAPER
B
BITS
C

IRAQI
ARABIC
NAMES
BITS
BITS
of CUT UP

PAPER

NAMES PAPER NAMES PAPER NAMES

IN
ARABIC
NAMES
Q
BITS

Palaces of Glass and Stone

Chihuly in Jerusalem

Though a man she's loved for fifty years is ill
she doesn't say I love you. Anyway he knows.

They call each other Sweetheart and My dear.
She talks about the spaces in the skies

beyond her windows where the towers were,
tells him I could predecease you. He laughs.

She's bought a pack of photographs of glass
set next to crenellated walls and under cypresses

in the Holy City, long curved forms
like horns of rams in Bible-tales,

like water-droplets just before they fall. Colors
to compel an unbeliever: translucent green

of foam-slashed seas, blurts and streaks
and blotches: smears of pigment stilled

on disks and bottles, all spilled
from the vast shining. A wild excess

of feeling moving through has left its breath
in edges pink as clematis or vulva, orbs

like ornament in liturgies, a blue so right
her mouth fills up with water. Stacked cubes

the green and white of glaciers; hues
never found in nature: tinctures of titanium

and zinc tint plumes like pollen-bearing grasses,
rounds of cobalt rolled to rest against stones

beneath permanent skies. She wants to give him
something, as if color were a gift of time. Glass

drawn bright from furnaces, spun and cooled,
goes solid. Iridescent opaque blue, ice-white,

sun-red. Everything that ever happened there lies
in the stones and textures sand: argument, belief

and slaughter, though everyone they happened to
has gone. She and the man were salt and grit

common chemicals and water, the flux and frit
of the subjunctive going on, impure and importuning.

At Masada

Desert stretches away in every direction
beneath the stony outcrop: despite your will
you can't escape its history, and you know,
regardless of the view, not endless.
Gold sands, caves where once upon a time
eremites and madmen. At one edge, like a hem
on ancient raiment, the Dead Sea splashes
its erratic blue, white chemical salts
not visible from here. Blood-soaked history
present in the sands, and absent,
like your own history, as if all your dead
had gathered in the gold and violent light
and you knew their endless wonder
at the world ongoing on these hot dry winds.

Forgiveness: an Abstract

suffering wrong

suffering

wrong

atonement

moral anger

resentment

vengefulness

hurt

rage

trust

distrust mistrust

forgiveness

unilateral

unconditional

conditional

partial

dismay
diminishment

fury

despair

dejection
discouragement
~~disheartenment~~

disillusion
dissolution

loss of heart
loss of hope

loss

wounds

time
feelings moving over time like water

like water

accident

attack
misuse
abuse
injury

wounds

apology
forgiveness

forgiveness

reciprocity
reconciliation
reparation
repentance
responsibility
restitution
reconsideration
reconstitution
restoration

retribution

burden

sympathy
imaginative indwelling

apology

truth

trust

ressentiment

offerings

amends

moral transformation

moral weight

burden

burden

guilt

violation

intention

degradation
depredation

wrongdoing

acceptance
apology

alteration

redemption

II

The Tiger in the Driveway

has escaped the carousel and stands chained
to the trunk of a dogwood in the suburbs
fourteen miles from New York. Bright
in his new coat of paint, stripes reproduce

his likeness, light and shade, less
dangerous. Across the street, nearly hidden
in dense brushy rhododendron, a bronze swan
glimmers in dots of light like rain or little mirrors,

like medallions. When the light's right they reflect
the tiger, broken into pieces, flattened, tamed.
She doesn't want to listen to his panting on hot days
but senses how the chain beneath his chin

chafes skin. Sympathy like light wind, stirs,
lifts feathers weighted with metal. Nights
she imagines he slides like shadow
to the beds upstairs. Driven out (he is always

driven out) he slips behind the fridge or stove
and like a house-cat hisses when the woman
sprinkles water on her plants and wets his clothes.
He misses his little blue jacket but not the saddle

with gold tassels and gilt trim, and he longs
for music, but not the children, climbing
and patting. Summer afternoons he dozes
in the shade of the garage–blades and spokes,

old bikes and broken mowers, kin beneath
their grime and dust, brown furry frosting.
He is wood and metal, marzipan
and manifest desire miraculously fashioned

into peaches, plums, tigers. His fine eyes blink
their green intelligence in all that dark
and when he stretches, pink tongue curling, bars
bend and heave: he is potential mouth and froth

and leap, brings smells like meat and scent
of muddy rivers with him: streaks, abrasions,
traces of tall grasses, dreams of fatty thighs
of swans, their gorgeous black splayed paddlefeet.

Tropes for the Unsayable
or
Shop of Last Hopes or Scent of Lilies

incipience: thought
before it makes itself available

path of river on the map
of how it is between us

shreddy-edged uneven rectangle
white lace
no bigger than a handkerchief

love's bloody straits
gone dry and stiff

the permanent denial
of the boy Isaac

certainty's dazzling
embrace and icy splendor

–after Clarice Lispector

A Loaf of Bread

I called him on the margins of his name
–Vallejo

Departures

Yet again I have spent my last
twenty-five dollars on a book of poems,
fat yeasty rolls warmed by hands
like these, lyric gatherings like coral,
that living substance that hardens,
as speech does, into some kind of reality.

The gods are just. I left one man,
another's leaving me. At the airport
in Atlanta, adrift in rhythms
past remedy or remembering, I'm closer
to R, whose southern sounds even Newark
couldn't harshen, J's too-easy invitations,
David the sharecropper's son. From filament
flung fluid till fine strands shine they spun
slender webs to catch the breath
in netted light and heavy air.

I play with stones, pile them up
in cairns, make corridors, doorways,
walls, light-shafts: architecture
of what I can't know
for people who have not arrived.

It was going to be grief, perfect
as ripe fruit, unblemished but longer lasting.
It was going to be peonies, thick
and dreamy, sweet as my thighs.

Life rolls forward heavy, stupefied
by increasing velocity. Perhaps bread
in stead of buildings. The slow
invisible movement of yeast animals
engendering something we can savor
but not save, bread
does not pretend to significance.

Arrivals

A recipe for loaves, time-worn and faithless:

for J: wildflowers dripping with color
and the wet from your mouth

for A: music that rises in your throat
and returns you to me
as to the clamor and necessity
of a holy city

For Don: awe
which is love, and rage
to bake them in

And for David, blood.

–for Don Hall

The Long Emptying

The swimming pool in sunlight:
water draining without noise
or your awareness over time,
the concrete streaked
and cracked and peeling. Children
pull strips of turquoise latex
from the walls and there it is,
stained and crumbling, that was all
a cup to hold the sun on water,
movement scattering
bright ornaments of light,
wavery pink quartz, green tourmaline,
that sweet gleam in the darkness
that glitter all your summer days.

Two Photographs

("W, March 2000, #12" and "W, March 2000, #3", Philip-Lorca diCorcia)

#12

The photograph's curved bar, pillars,
and the way the light's laid on, echo
Nighthawks, and oppose it. Also night.
Beyond a pane of glass, the face
of a bartender slightly turned away
repeats the face of one of two men playing
mirror-games, hands up and joined–
prefiguring the way they'll come together.
Through another opening–doorway?–
a young woman lights the shadowy
interior, one red-shod foot on the edge
of the bar's stone base. Her cigaret case,
or perhaps a little silver purse, winks
white and satiny from the dark recess,
like her silhouette: buttock, one taut thigh,
outlined in a skin-tight green-lit dress.

#3

The woman sits on a bed in a cheap room
high above a city, refiguring *Morning Sun.*
Her pink striped shirt–perhaps it's textured–
repeats and varies horizontal blinds
along the wall at the back (that is, top)
of the image, wide window through which
we see the reach of the city and the fading day.
A tall building restates hard verticals
of her upright posture. Like Jo in 1952
her weight makes almost no impression
on cream-colored patterned chenille
though shadows like ink-stains extend
her still presence. All the perturbation
is interior. Jo leans forward a bit,
toward the window, in her bright pink slip.
This figure is not waiting, expects nothing.

Each Day a Sacrament

Dear Blue-Denim kin. Some days grief
swings in, brief visit from the augury
with wide wingspan who circles
like the pelican returning to 9th floor windows
where my brother and I watched tides
while our father lay dying, as if
we'd needed a reminder. Time

takes whom it will and when, and I
need your radically different language
daily giving voice to mysteries,
friendship ordinary on its surfaces
as stones in sun, delivered here by chance
or fallen or uplifted, each itself only.

Heaved by forces older than imagination, each
wears or weathers in its own way, and we
call them all the same plain sturdy name: stone.

–for Chet Frederick

A Late Appreciation, Mostly Marine-Blue

The seven minutes on a ferry between Gotland and Fårö, sunlit water
in the narrow strait the perfect heart of blue

a poem you read when you were seventeen, an embrace
at night on a beach, the first man you leaned into fully

the proposal you didn't hear, the proposition you scorned

hauling yourself through time and tall wet grasses
uphill over rocky scarps, crossing broken slabs
of wide pink stone to a wind-scourged tidal island
facing icy seas

the men who asked you what you needed
when you were a net of pure raw need
or gave you what you needed
when you didn't know its name
or that you needed it, did not know
how to ask, or could not

a moment will be altering your life and you won't know for decades

which were crevasses from which you could never have been rescued
and which gifts, bright apples, scented, grainy in the mouth
their warm sweet water dripping
down the thin skin of your inner arm

At the North Sea

–57° 41' N, Scotland

Stony, lichen-spattered, land falls to inlets,
coves, fjords, odd gaps where chunks of earth
pulled away by currents leave scarps streaked
with the remains of little animals and seaweed
daily battered by the waves. At the end of the world
for the first time a clutch of humans gather, unable
to lift their eyes from the moving and terrible body of light.

One, having watched the shoals of great and little fish,
squats, extends a hand to taste it that first time,
the sun low in a sky streaming blood and promise.
One dreams the first currach, builds a little craft
and hot with terror runs on slick stones into shallows,
icy recognition filling throat and chest with cries,
heaves himself athwart the edge, sets sail.

Stone Circle

Loanhead, Daviot
Aberdeenshire

High above a valley golden with ripe barley, houses
clinging to the hills, we come upon a wide stone circle,
gritty unmarked central plane ringed by swaths
of rubble, all enclosed by upright granite kerbs, echoes
of the milestones on old Roman roads nearby.
Bronze Age sacred fires tossed sparks on winter skies,
leaving infant skulls, scorched bones. What changes?
Down through time it seems the eye is pleased
by circles within circles–shimmering unstable discs
of water and ring-compasses of stone. We strode
the canted surface stroking granite freckled by dark minerals
and mica and the dried white excrement of birds, enclosed,
excluded. Watchstones' immediate plurals tell something,
and leave out everything: the abject and exalted,
all that ordinary fluid thrust and recoil of the living.

–for Gayle and Joffy

Icefall

1

Scrawls of Greenland snow: runes of sea-green
blues on wind-honed stone. Once upon a time
–had anyone been there to see–wave
on wave of trembling green to the horizon: trees.

In North America ice-sheets lay a mile deep.

Ice-core slices tell days a hundred-thousand years ago:
rain, volcanic ash, snow. Bits of bark and pine, dust
and wind-borne seeds. Seashells, soot, remains
of tiny skeletons and inorganic grit.

Electric sheets unfold from solar wind,
Aurora's spangled draperies flickering
like mind, a fully articulated idea
sweeping past before you catch it, soft flash
of momentary light in all that dark. Pitiless
as memory the glacier shows how time stops,
solids move, the heart's flux goes.

2

Today in high seas, temperatures below zero
and winds which made rescue impossible
the search for a young Norwegian who fell
into a crevasse in an effort to bring out
Amundsen's remaining effects was abandoned.

That last deliberate step
heart's lurch
before the fall
like the pilot
of a plane in stall:
perfect knowledge.

As if a line–like thought, tightrope, lifeline–
had been tossed across the house of dread
and rapture and gone taut. It spins, thins
strand by strand. He must've called out
to the others *Go!* before sleep in implacable cold.

3

In high country I drank glacial runoff mixed
with snow-melt. Clear over multicolored stones
the water tasted white and elemental in its granite bowl,
blue cirque silver and reflective. Blue as the heart
of the sky, the glacier seems still. Within,
corridors and caves, channels ice-worms carve,
and pocked walls tilted, warped and faulted.

4

After the glacier a swath of erratics
like civilizations in ruins. As after lava.
Hot or frozen, regardless, the land lies stunned
in the wake. So I, after you go.

Dead Reckoning

The position of a ship determined by calculations
from previous position, direction, speed, and time.
Error is greater in turbulent weather.

His vessel splintered in the ice, unaware
of the Rising at home, Shackleton

pushes off a scree-strewn spit with six men
to cross eight hundred miles of Southern Ocean

in the twenty-foot *James Caird.* The grid
we've pitched over the world says Easter, 1916.

Icebergs roll in squalls as if they didn't weigh
ten thousand tons, and numbers matter:

climate bending light brings mountain ranges
closer than it's safe to figure from, and time slips

knots around event and anchors it to place.
They are at sea for sixteen days. Swells

wrench the rudder off into the waves; they lose
fifty feet of alpine rope, the drogue–a cone of canvas

rigged to catch the wind–the skipper's boots,
and sleeping bags that haven't dried for seven months.

On the day they peel the sealskin trousers
from their thighs, wide strips of flesh

come with them. Time folds and shifts:
forward to the end of the century, East coast,

North America, the men's extremity reduced
to books and exhibition, sketches by McNeish,

a wooden box marked *Herdman, Edinburgh:*
Flour Millers to the King, and I can walk

the *James Caird's* length in nineteen steps.
Beneath great trees in sun I study journals

of their days. Satellites will not be built
for tens of years and they're without a radio.

Their lives have spiralled out like lines tossed
onto space and mine declines from the zenith,

years of blood between my legs, and men,
babies' heads on milk-hard breasts. As if

lifted from a medieval tapestry, a girl
in a sheer flowered dress swings by, and I

might be a tree, dark-rooted, leafy, stopped.
Like the men with Shackleton I've lost

everything I would have sworn was necessary
and life a gust so short it thwarts the heart.

Easy in her cloak as light as thought, the girl
strides on into her future and my past. Beyond

the reaches of her mind engaged by every flickering,
her age, as near to me as now. She doesn't see me

reading in the sun, a smudge, a brief sharp flare of light,
a tree that one day falls to earth, provisioning.

III

The Prose Middle

A Meditation on Bashō's *The Narrow Road to the Interior*

Narrow Road to the Interior: vagina:
Way in. Central passage, road, pathway, course,
corridor, transit, channel, aisle, conduit,
opening, portal (I love *portal*). Thesaurus: "part of a text."
I am the text.

Scored by surgeries I gazed at the East River for 26 days
and couldn't care.

There's a river here, across the street. Beyond,
as an image rises on photographic paper,
another town emerges
when leaves fall.

In the hospital I tried to count boats and notice what kinds:
yachts and tugs and garbage scows. Kayaks. Pleasure-craft,
people sunbathing on their decks. Here I haven't seen anything
on the river but light and shadow. No birds.
There must be birds.

I took Milosz's *Facing the River* to Scotland:
I'd read almost all of it before I realized the river he knew
in childhood was Lethe now that he was old.

How long it takes me to know anything.

There's a certain grain of stupidity that the writer
... can hardly do without, and this is the quality
of having to stare, of not getting the point at once.

Credulity's to blame. It has slowed the tragectory
(yes) of my work.

East River, Wabash, Lethe. Like a necklace, the silver shining
beads of their names. Rivers I've walked across, seen or been
on: Yellowstone, Thames, Seine, Delaware, Hudson, Charles,
Esk, Amstel, Lagan, Liffey, Spey. The Water of Leith. Streams
cutting into Stockholm, Copenhagen, Helsinki.

November morning, trees stripped. I watch a train's reflection
in the river, little rectangular chunks of light move between
dark blotches, as if the metal thing had lost materiality.

The Narrow Road to the Interior could just as faithfully be
mouth, eyes. Country roads and rutted tracks. Passages
and footpaths past strawberry fields and tomatoes in
Oneco, through palmetto fields and orange groves, across
cornfields on the way to Chicago, houses tucked away in
folds of northern California hills–no trees. Little private
roads to shacks in mountains, summer places buried
in dunes, houses up on concrete blocks,
structures we spend our lives in made of dreams.

How things are erased. After the hospital I couldn't read for
four months.

Desert winds' erasures. In Jerusalem
I lifted bowls with both hands:
all the fruit smelled like flowers.

And grief's: After my mother died, I couldn't read for a year.

White stone, dry air, flowers.

Growing things I knew from childhood, bougainvillea,
oleander. Croton. Traveler's palm, date palms heavy with fruit,
banana plantations.

Golden sand at Masada,
the history of blood.

Oasis: astonishment of green and water.

Bitter poisonous Dead Sea. Cave dwellings high in hills.

In the Sinai–I am told–the desert is a different color, and more
stones. There the desert fathers made icons brilliant even now,
a thousand years from when they painted them.

Across the Jordan, watchtowers. I waved.
The other people on the tour quit talking to me.

Borders: lines in the imagination and the body politic. Two Irelands, Koreas, Chinas, Vietnams. Dakotas. When I was nine I expected palms and sandy beaches when the sign said
Welcome to Florida!

Land mines.
The Troubles are infinite and everywhere.

Where I live now there's rust in the water but no irony.

I need *city,* energy fizzing up from plural angles, ways of being, languages.

Irony's urban, though not only,
& characteristic of the twentieth century
where I will have lived most of my life.

And irony muffles, distorts; is *interesting.*

Actually, I have written down my experience in the closest detail.
But the rough and vulgar facts are not there.

Four years after the event, a singular true image:

I am a giant redwood tree. Men stand to my right
and left, legs braced. They swing wide their axes,
thwack! thwack! thwack! into soft white thighs.

IV

Winter

Battered after surgeries I tread earth like stone
prowling nurseries for plants I know
from days a thousand miles from here: sweet droop
of banana leaves, gardenias' mad excess.
Oleander, clematis. Like music names come back
–shock of scarlet bougainvillea familiar
after half a century–color's note a tone
you couldn't fail to recognize, like strings'.
Soft clatter of bamboo. Scent of earth allays
as wasn't possible in days of perpetual summer.
Beyond knowledge, knowing: this
is where I'm going. I choose cut blooms
whose stalks go bronze in heavy rains, peonies,
their soft mop-heads bees' wildest fantasies.

Petals drift for days onto my tables and my floors
as if a mythic bird had been my visitor.

What Takes Us Down

The weight, as of seas heaped with swells,
of history streaked with Baltic tourmaline, rose
quartz and cobalt seamed with gold, pyrite
sparkling here and there along galleries of dark
that go all the way back to the beginning
–perhaps beyond. Evil witnessed
and imagined, tides of vengeful wishes
those you know have told you, intermittent
showers of malice and all you do not say.
You thought it was Time. It is
these that crease flesh, loosen its hold
on your bones. These, wind in wild grasses,
creatures' silver flickerings through groundwater
bearing blood and breath our Time is made of.

Oxen, Harnesses

Oxen lean into their traces, press and pull.
Hail strikes their backs, lightning prickles hide,

thunder drums the bones in their shoulders.
They drag great weight, plough fields, move sheds

and trees and boulders. Heads down, in pairs
or teams or singly they do as they are bidden.

She wonders if they dream of running, dream of grass.
Film clips from the century just past show people

gathered in the squares, massed in streets,
marching, chanting, banners broad and bright.

There were Partisans, refuseniks, revolutionaries
in Beijing, Bucharest, Santiago and New York.

Young men burned to death outside Johannesburg
and starved in Northern Ireland's jails.

Shot, beaten, stacked and shoveled into pits, the dead
and the alive together. Walls were built and fell.

Consider China and the North of Britain: outlanders
will get in anyway. She wants to know how torturers

can kiss their wives and children, how wives can have them;
how they can sleep. Like a great bird–dirty, beautiful

in flight–Gandhi's news flew all the way from India
to North America because we needed it.

Do you remember youngsters at lunch-counters
in her South and the terrible trees?

Everywhere in villages and little towns and granite
cities, people reached and stretched, said *No*. Now she.

Closed systems: manifestations of evil.

▴

Irony throws a cloak over the heart.

▴

All control is illusory.

▴

Declarations of love without acts: yellow flower bent to the pool, gazing.

▴

Time circles us like death, which is one of its attributes.

Visit

Hotel room. I eat breakfast in the city
in which somewhere you rise and stretch,
do things in the bathroom, kiss
your wife. If you don't know I'm here
I'm not. Like the figure in a photograph
a friend described: stood the camera
on a stone ledge in an empty church, fixed
the time-exposure for low light and waited.
Art requires patience. The long draft
of your love, like oceans'–as if the world
drew breath–the froth and rush
of its unstoppable return. Developed,
the image shows a figure spun from spume
and foam on her knees before the altar.

Interior, Gulf Coast

Sun-slammed, the glass box in a series of such boxes
looks out on tops of trees, royal palms in colonnade,
high hot-weather clouds and sawgrass, sun's hieroglyphs
on water. They are alone here, the man on the phone
talking money. He is very ill and she's afraid. She jots
Devotion's love in chaste and common clothing.
He is incurious and entirely courteous, a fine contrast
to his ferocity in bed. What will happen to them? Everything
has already happened.

She looks up to joists and struts
obscured by ceiling-tile and panelling, thinking
of the great cathedrals, men bent beneath the weight of stone
in early dark, erratic leaping light from braziers, slings
and pulleys, the lifting and the scaffolding, slow press
of oxen in their braces, shapes of gratitude, apparatus of belief.

A Change of Heart

She couldn't possibly have married him
but she has learned the code he speaks
and sometimes she can speak it. His call

as from a distant continent, lurid sound
on early-morning dark: *I'm 1-A*
on the transplant list. Or *A-1.*

She slips between *now* and a series of thens,
some fifty years old–his heartbeat
trembling the bones of her cheek: hotel rooms,

Gulf-coast beaches. On her way
to Quebec, the opposite direction, she waits
for a plane amid flurries of slang,

a high-school choral group bound home.
If they spoke English she might be diverted
but these are periodic nouns abloom

in slushy sibilants. She drifts. Strands
of song like aural spiderweb cross airport space,
design of truth beyond what he could say,

the last loved man, who's known her
broken, open. She resonates to his struck *A*
across the thousand miles. One day she heard

a group of EKGs transcribed as quarter-notes,
laid on staves and played: strong hearts sing
ornamented melodies, sick hearts plain lines

like early chants. All over the world
people are going places and he lies as if dead,
a man with a hole in his chest.

Rhythmic slosh of pumps thuds
under engine-noise. Time *zings* and pools.
She imagines fever charts and what she knows

will happen does. She isn't family. The nurses
will refuse to speak and he will not be able to.
She's never been the other woman.

She's been the one before, between, and after.
She comes to know *to be beside oneself*
and tells herself in the third person

She chose not to be with you so she can't
be with you. Years go. For a time
they lived through days without each other,

a bright sweet silent phosphorous
streaming through the shallows of familiar seas,
soft breezes over tropic nights and terror.

–In Memory, RPR

Future Present

Future is what happens after.
Once upon a time in a distant land
there were certainties formal
as geometries. Dazzled, I took him
in his narrow bed, broke
open everything. What follows is.

City

When the bus swings to the curb and stops
with that heavy sigh anybody could be on it.

The ghost of your grandfather, bringing
back sweet smell of his cigars whose red-gold
paper bands were your first jewelry. A man
you loved, wandering the vast yards
of the dead. A younger self, more whole
and more accomplished–and more beautiful–
than you could know. A suicide bomber.

New York, wrapped copper-gold at sunset,
turquoise, apricot and pink at dawn.
From where I live a scrawl of blue or gray, graph
or fever-chart, depending on the light.
The missing buildings.

In the Medieval Sculpture Hall

–Concert, Music for Solace, late September 2001
for David, Richard, Adele, Yaddo, 1981

You pull open boxes, lift out gray blocks,
slice them with fine thread–spiderweb

if you have it–and lay them, sheet upon sheet
up the walls all the way to the windows.

Shipped from Canterbury in heavy cartons
and bent during the crossing, this light

must be flattened to fit the American space.
Bright sounds unspool before the Spanish gates

and when the music ends we drop
into our lives again to find, gathered in archways

and doorframes, before altarpieces and reliquaries, clots
of silent people have drawn close to one another

and been listening. A cradle in a glass box
gleams like a pond spattered with moonlight

and on a nearby table-top, a small gold triptych
from old brutal Germany or France. Players

and audience disperse, leaving all this
weightless light, these girls of wood and stone

besotted by their babies, Madonnas
from the Low Countries, the Mary from Asturias.

Like her I was ungathered fruit. Her dress
bright swoops of sunny color trimmed with blues

like fallen sky, she wears a garland swagged
with blossoms. In hills across the sea

a sun-brown man bent to the olivewood.
Earth-stained careful hands carved thighs, dared

the soft swell of her breasts, fashioned ornament,
and fixed her hair in whorls, seedpods, acorns.

View with Water and Prepositions

The sky today's a perfect level ceiling
over rooms of hills and trees.
Wild and cultivated patches
show where we have been. Cloud lies

over   before   above   in front   outside of
near   around   a city. Within
sometimes.   Upon   or   toward but not
underneath   and   also   because of   perhaps.

Today's March 3rd '02: I have to know
where I am, what day it is. There has to be
a river, ocean, city–preferably New York–
to the east. As at Boston and Dublin, wide plain
of water under sunrise where the city leans
like a mammoth, tangled fur studded with burrs
and excrement dragging against stones to drink.

The Palace at 4 AM

Two-year-old Ruth wants to know
Do you have a sunroom?

No.

That's okay. The men
will bring you one. An idea
full as the palace at 4 AM
through which events drift
like swags of pale chiffon,
snag now and then
on an upright or cling
with some deliberation
to the occasional horizontal.

I wander through, needing voices
–my mother's especially–

remembering loved men, islands
low in cold green seas, deserts,
windswept high country,
cloudforms, tropic skies,
scent of gardenias, long roads
through orange groves.

I Go Home

The boy in a white dinner-jacket
who pressed against me on a moonlit night
beside the Gulf is seventy, old man
in silk slacks. We walk the sand
and do not touch, our hands
aware of one another When we join
filling the abyss as time has filled it
we will tumble raw and young as if
we do not know how much we have
to lose on parting. As if
we rode a pair of mythic horses
over plains filled with the shining ordinary
on which we float as once the world
was said to float, on a vast sea, and does:
seas of time and place which are one thing
and when we are together everything.

Circus

Children of aaaaall aaages! She knows
the years of training in the heat, grit
ground into skin, immigrants whose every hope

rides on the horses, with the drums.
Heavy smells of camels. Girdled stallions
prance in circles to the liquid whoops

of the calliope thirty blocks north of where
–once upon a time–the Towers stood.
Dancing spots light loops of greasy rope,

toss insubstantial apparatus onto air, guywires
taut to tent-top. Three rings. Which may be
how to think about the past, and memory, and now.

She wouldn't have them back, the bright
unshadowed places of her girlhood, hard marriage,
dead child. Up in the rigging, tow-lines, nets

and ropes, and all of it unnatural:
when the man in the cage with the tigers runs
they do not spring to catch him but arc

like burning liquid through his hoops–
she thinks about obedience, its value and its toll.
Above the center ring the wide net floats

like history, catches light and time, and holds.
Beautiful uneducated hopeless brave, girls
in high-heeled strappy shoes parade

on elephants, waving sweetly, as plants
move underwater and in dreams. Swayed
by time and currents they are glorious

in bodies such as she herself had once,
had she but known it. Spangled, splashed
with glitter, red-tasselled satins stretch

to cover breasts and bottoms. Thighs splayed
to straddle the great beasts are thick,
well-muscled. She gazes at their shiny golden shoes.

The Old Woman Tells You Things

Others' indifference is teaching her silence—or she's practicing.
Sometimes she thinks *Old women are so gallant!*
They don't throw themselves into traffic at 86th and Fifth.
No one would choose to be flimsy, forgetful. No one
would choose loose flesh and illness. Grit
crumbles to particles: these are her bones. Sometimes
she wonders if, fierce in her youth, she strode unseeing
past old women. This would be a kind of justice.
None of this has she chosen, except insofar as she's here,
facing the long corridor, curved at the end, and no door.

It Begins

as accident, becomes necessary, becomes art,
and how you know is it makes you hungry,
makes it possible to recognize something
in the embryonic green deformed
sweet pepper in its bright red-orange
parent when you cut it for your salad.

Music you have never heard, remember
in detail, can sing, anticipating every chord-change,
every modulation. It tells you who you are.
Not the high-school girl who stubbornly holds on,
carousing, dreaming, not that nascent self,
and not the wife, mother, sister, daughter, lover.
Some other woman you have never seen and know
with perfect clarity: with her you find yourself
at home and easy in the unexplained.

–for Sandra Daniel

The Limits

move like a device that probably does not exist
but I imagine sliding on the horizontal
as on oiled track, silent, steady,
like one of those machines that presses cars
into heavy dense small chunks.
I am trying to say how the limits fix
the space between you and what you want,
the thing you need. Crush space but fail
to bring you closer. The vertical plate
drives forward on its metal plane
without intention or malice, twinkling
as it comes, and wholly without pity.

Saint George and the Dragon

Framed by brick vaults, watched over
by a painted Queen of Heaven, daily
Saint George slays a dark reticulated dragon
at Storkyrkan, Stockholm. Daily
vanquished, his fitted plates of mother-of-pearl
catch sharp glints through stained glass.
Over time men have navigated by the stars,
knowledge of the currents near home-islands,
angles of the sun. Now my friend George, pilot
of planes and sailing vessels, hiker, poet,
student of terrain and languages and wildflowers,
calls me daily in the hospital. He will not leave me
with the brutalized and maimed. Or:
leaves me, his voice a blaze on trails to days
beyond vexed stillness and the strange.

–for George Petty

Here, After

–Hall of Evolution, American Museum of Natural History

My son pushes my wheelchair
through rooms drenched in Time

past glass-caged remains
of Homo sapiens and a range

of antecedents: so many
dead ends, so many

fruitless branchings of the tree.
Strings of bones gleam

where light strikes.
When did we begin to dream?

Wrapped in local and familiar time
we are not thinking *Time,*

obdurate, invariant, that lays event
against event till all the past

is one long endless *then.*
When did we begin to expect

a future? Forty years ago,
singing little songs, I drove

his stroller, held him safe
in scary places. Children

stream past dragging
parents forward. We roll

into our own time and through.
Once upon a time I strode.

The Gate at Visby, I

Memory is at the gate and waves time through.

Bright July and full of wind. The girl
climbs steep hills toward the wall,

skip-runs under the portcullis
and out onto wild fields where boys

bring cattle for sweet summer grass.
Breathless with the running, driven

to explore—unwilling to obey the rules
that only men go—alone, she goes

beneath blowing trees and high blue skies.
Eight hundred years in the future

an aging woman will heave herself up
the seventy-two stone steps beside

double-spired Domkyrkan S:ta Maria
where the girl sat watching builders

laughing in the sun and wrestling stone.
Days are twenty hours long in summer

and full, like grown-up days, of consequence.
Struggling for breath the woman climbs

toward medieval walls, stone crenellations
cut-outs on the sky, and turrets

flying flags like those in picture-books,
aware that walls have always failed

to keep the stranger out. Astonished
by the effort and by hymns she knows

from childhood in Florida returned to marry
words in Swedish on blue sun-crossed air,

she hauls reluctant bones above the sea,
thinking of the boats, how men have always

sailed away and home with new wives,
booty, spices and belief, since the girl,

scrambling through tall tangled grasses,
over stones. She lives fully in the present,

can't imagine a museum in the woman's time,
the gathering of picture-stones that tell

her people's history. Ignoring scrapes,
arms scored by branches, she climbs,

slowed now by weight, her apron full
of early apples. For a time the old one

stood at the grave of a *thirty-year-old woman,*
late stone age, the beautiful small bones

of her feet returning to earth, a heap
of little cylinders repeating shapes

of whistles at her head. The woman studied
a seal-figurine of fired clay, a comb,

the short imagined life. Heedless of wind
on her limbs the girl toils over scrub

and rough terrain as night comes on,
runs hard, hard, her chest hurts. Within

the gate in her faraway time, the woman
bends to roll two blue-gray coverlets into bolsters

on her narrow bed, stops to gaze out over rooftops
to the swells and shadows of the darkening sea.

Idly, a soft cloth in hand, she rubs
five bright green apples till they shine.

The Gate at Visby, II

Narrow Swedish-blue room, single bed
at one end, summer quilts rolled at head
and foot beneath a window on the Baltic,
blue and gray and green and scored
by sails like crests of waves to the horizon:
the July regatta. *Sommar! Sommar!*
Ljuva Sommar! On the sill a small white bowl,
its rim like a cuff, holds five bright apples.
When she looks out over red tile rooftops
down steep terraces to sea, sun and wind
in her face, she imagines winter's cargo,
cloud low with ice and snow
streaming north toward Finland,
a girl running, heart churning
like an angry sea: *The gate–*
Tumbling over stones and branches,
tripping in tall grass and over roots,
she cannot outrun terror: there will be
boars and wolves and wild dogs:
Christ bring me home before it closes!

V

Lineac

—acronym: linear accelerator

You only have to see a brief stretch
you only have to see it once.
Like an earthquake or tornado
no one needs a second time.
Inter-galactic freight train
someone said, structures
she recalls gray-white, half-buried
in the hills outside Palo Alto
strung like boxcars
at oblique angles to each other
and the road, like a sketch
for derangement, figure for odd turns
and quirks in one you love, the arc
of strangeness in yourself, sheen
of particles at speed, sun-white
antic blue, electric green.

Hill, Stone, Stream

Where do they go, sticks and struts and slabs
of stories told to one now dead? He took them
with him into earth, which remembers nothing
and keeps everything. Burial along fracture-lines
does not deter the men who bury atomic waste
in its glass cages, giant bottles I imagine green.
One day the earth will heave and split,
the glass open, and words will stream
like rivers though the rock, pour dark red, streaks
like iron laid ten million years ago along a scarp,
or copper, bearing scraps of marvelous harmonics,
break the surface, toss their glitter on the air.
Particles might snag in the serrated edges of a leaf
or blow like pollen caught in crevices in trees, or spin
up into cloud and gather till they fall again with rain.

Notes from a Bicycle Trip with Marianne Moore in Rock Springs, Wyoming

1

So MM and I are tooling along, pedal and glide,
the surrounds like hills in O'Keeffe paintings
–the ones with all the black–and teleological
US-green road signs that don't say where you are
but just how far, when under the Route 80 overpass
where trucks slow before they clamor on toward New York
or San Francisco, we pause to animate dry country:
blackberry bushes, and a river pouring by,
salmon streaming up it toward the Great Divide
which like a child I want to see as one sees roads
from air, fine lines laid on land, Mason
and Dixon, the Equator, borders of nations; lines
defining settlements and language, signs
reminding you of all those yellow lamps you see
from planes in isolated houses, as if by planting trees
in rows or building, we could occupy
and having occupied, be comforted.

2

These are days when if you look with care
you can see great loves
being lived out in the lives of your friends.

3

Everybody's going to Budapest and China.
Reports come back from places closed
for most of the last century, and all of us
are living consequences of choices
made with insufficient information.

4

In the tropics where I was a girl, before the local battering
sounds rush up the streets with a *whoosh* like palm-fronds'
sweep and *swush*, walls of water whiten air.

Didion says weather's easy. Not when it's extreme:
Jakarta in monsoon, the slam and weight and steam
of water in the air, and trees black-green.
Dusk shines all day in the peculiar creamy air,
a color like gardenias but without the scent.
Rot and mold bloom like tigers.

Bow before the rains.

5

In the quiet after, you can hear enchantment:
the noise that moment makes
when the bravest and most beautiful
of the twelve dancing princesses breaks
one silver leaf from the bough and its voice
sends strands of glitter on the wind.
Who has seen the wind? Neither you nor I,
But when the trees bow down their heads, the wind!
is passing by. Here in the desert no trees
to make it visible, the wind unrolls out of the west
like a prehistoric lizard-tongue designed
for tearing things in two. Sign says Evanston
119 miles. Not Illinois and I forget in which direction.

Labyrinth

A woman follows a gold thread through the night
past raw walls oozing sticky color, rubs a bit
on her finger, taps the finger to her lower lip: light
tongue-touch. Sweet and salty, metallic, like blood,
taste of gems gone liquid, small savory delight
above the trap-door to the tigers and the blameless dark.

Paul's House

We walk along the river saying so little
it's as if nothing's happening. Loss
lays dark blots between the trees, shadows

text and anti-text, his wife, his other
woman, the man I loved it would've ruined me
to marry. Indoors little buildings, wire

skeletons for cloth, stand around waiting
to be realized. Gold light zings off the water, swarms
of silent jeweled insects flung onto panels

of green velvet fixed here and there
to rough wood walls. His houses all
have odd small windows, and they brim

with light. Today it trembles the water
like memory–he shows the mark: on a post
above our heads a stain records how high

the water rose when it swept in
and would have drowned his son
had something not awakened him.

Doors and Time

My daughter leaves. We turn from one another.
She flings herself onto the world and something in me closes,
its last uses over. Trees grow tall and flower

bringing color into leafy canopies. With her brothers
she rushes toward a future I won't see. Close
my eyes. When as we must we turn from one another

I want the grace–hands up and open–my mother
brought to times like these. Times close.
My daughter leaves. Trees grow tall and flower.

At ten she'd call me to the mirror, laughter
squinting shut her eyes: I look like you! So close.
I failed to see. We turn from one another

and it's good for her that we're so different. Lovers
come into her foreground. Doors close.
My daughter leaves. Sunlit trees grow tall and flower.

Nothing's lost. Phosphorescent seas, my daughter,
and starry spatterings on midnight skies will close
around you when my arms have gone to light. Leave.
We turn from one another. Trees grow tall. They flower.

Great-Grandmother Comes to Me in a Dream

carrying sprigs of white and yellow wildflowers trailing
leaves she is perhaps eighteen sunlight streams

onto fine hair brown-red a few curls falling from blue ribbons
trimmed with white strides wide fields years

before her limbs open bring out seven children
some of whom won't grow Lithe light

small bony feet restrained by little boots made
extravagance! for this visit Invitation

undreamed of So she comes by train
more than one-hundred-fifty versts farthest

she will ever be from Moscow to this house outside Tula
Sofia Andreyevna's house where–voices crossing one another

laughing – they picked the flowers she is holding
Sofia Andreyevna Mother's friend seen last

before my ancestor's womanhood came on wife now
to an older man *he writes books!* she cannot read

At a table set out under trees cucumbers in sour cream
with crusty bread and cheese borscht a chilled delicious

pleasure on the summer day and ah her friend's fine welcome
great house and pretty children The man walking

with his secretary book in hand stops breath
she'd thought a writer would be polished

like a city-man Though rough
in countenance he comes to greet her gently and with warmth

Servants bring the samovar sweet tea as light fades
in the corner of the drawing room Sofia Andreyevna favors

Flowers tumble from a blue enamel vase
edge of gold braid and table dressed

with patterned cloth from somewhere far away East?
On the walls faces distract Her people do not permit

images Sofia Andreyevna has begun work
in a new science making pictures she calls photographs shows

children and Lev Nicolaevich on the steps of the house
and you can see the orchards –points–

weren't yet fully grown In all directions dark
beyond tall windows endless wood cut by paths

her husband likes to walk with his dogs she says
glad of solitude and trees birdcall scents

of earth and growing things Light a pale smear
on the sky they show her a bed under the vaults

She lies alone in greeny light In years to come
she'll dream the older couple's marriage its ease

and golden plates and serving people beautiful children
vast reaches of forest ponds with reedy edges

fine for bathing   green wood a comforting enclosure
Winter nights she will remember   Sofia Andreyevna

and her man in summer evening light   hips touching
on the red silk sofa   his fine eyes her eloquence

in French and Russian   words in German
an accomplishment   She will lie in bed

and hope for plenty   if not riches like her friend's
a good man to share her bed   though she can't know

how men and women are together   how daily lives
burn and brim with grief and laughter   Simple girl

she has no idea   what love is   One day she will make milk
for babies she has given birth to and for orphaned others   she

imagines none of this   and cannot imagine   me
in a faraway country   at ease in my difficult language

centuries having turned   and turned again
nor does she know how germ cells wrapped in helical embraces

bearing gait and eye-shape   hers and mine   will spill
down and down and down through unimagined time

Perhaps Chimes

The child at the window patient as a tree
is half-obscured by dense green shrubbery
and vivid as a paper doll before a plane

of purest black, the dark implastic. An odd
and quiet smile shows knowledge unavailable
to four-year-olds. She doesn't blink or nod.

As after a struck tone a strident silence
spills down time and into a wide vacancy.
The child's presence says the woman's died.

Clouds cross windless skies, blue returns,
flushed apricot and rose. The child
dissolves in daylight. Briefly skies

hold sorrow as the calyx holds the flower.
The woman gazes at empty space,
and like water after turbulence goes still.

Island of the Dead

Arnold Böcklin, Swiss (1827-1901)

O yes. Recognition opens on a breath,

the river dark, and figures in the boat
–ferryman, passenger–facing away
from the viewer, drenched with light.

They gaze into a lighted slot in stone.
What happens if you haven't coins to pay
and the use of alder bark by Roman legions

to write letters home hasn't happened yet?
Everything happens, Russian fables say,
In a land long ago and far away. The strait,

broad near us, but narrowing, goes
into the dark, a wood of course, beyond
where we can see. We know they will go

through, and imagine the passenger
is one of the Thirty-six Just Men who live,
in Hassidic tales, at all times, somewhere

in the world: they don't know who they are;
like us they do what's next: approach
the narrow gates of stone, go through.

Sarcophagus

Head on a pillow unyielding as a bolster
she wonders if she'd joined them
–what had it been like those days and nights
she'd lain with princes, knights in armor, even poets–
what was it to have been dead, like Mary
Queen of Scots, whose head had been taken.
How would she sleep? Remembered impulse
skitters down arms, through fingers. She wants
to brush dust that like water has gathered
in low places, notches at clavicle and sternum, dip
in the philtrum, little pit at the base of the spine.
      Weight of lids on carved marble boxes
            containers for forgetting.

Geometries of Absence

1

Peter Voulkos' nearly impossible mass
of clay taller than a man and round,
immense silent gong masquerading
as rough stone, solitary in the room
and dark. Nothing else exists.

2

In the quiet middle of the night
when I'm looking through a window
at the moon, clouds streaming
over its face, the sound of a plane.
We say *from nowhere.* In fact
a place unknown or unexpected.
When sound has gone, the plane's
still there. It's like this with the dead
who poke their fingers through space-time,
touch us with scent or sound.

3

Because your arms were unavailable,
death being unavailing, I slept in a circle
of moonlight and when in shallow sleep
I drifted up to wakefulness
–as in mirrors people moving toward us
seem to float up to the surface of the glass–
I turned in the cool insubstantial embrace
as when all night I knew your flesh, sweet weight.

4

When you've been called awake by church bells
–chimes like aural glitter–you can't know
how many have tolled and if another tone
will fill the waiting. Silence moves
like the upward inflection in speech,
not quite question. No answer.

(On Not) Believing in an Afterlife

Terrase Dufferin, Québec, on my birthday

This easy day I can't imagine the St. Lawrence
under heaped and broken slabs of ice or driven,

gray beneath the Northern Lights. Our tour-boat's
dwarfed by the ice-cutter *Amundsen*, bright emblem

of extremity in red and white, her ensigns shivering
in gusts of summer westerlies. In months to come

I will appear in strangers' photographs, the figure
no one noticed then, woman at the edge, white blur

facing water or the sky–a life without a text
brought home to Saskatoon or Seoul. Thus

I move about the world. Success! Einstein said
if you could travel fast enough you wouldn't age.

Seashells, foreign stones and images: I collect
names of places I will never see, Christchurch,

Madagascar, Kenya, Chile's ice-green seas,
Straits of Magellan. Strait: isthmus in negative.

I want to leave without looking back, to go
as I have always gone, mostly unafraid, gaze direct,

hands open in momentum gathering like wind,
leaning onto the perilous blue: *What next?*

Notes

"Icefall"

The italicized section is from a radio broadcast, no date

"Forgiveness, an Abstract"

Much of the language is from "A Sorry Business," Charles L. Griswold's Review of *Resentment's Virtue,* Thomas Brudholm; *I Was Wrong,* Nick Smith; and *Making Amends,* Linda Radzik: *TLS* (Jan. 7, 2011, 28).

Ressentiment: undoing of the past: the translation is Griswold's.

"The Prose Middle"

Recovering from violence to her spirit, breast cut away, a poet-friend read Kimiko Hahn's *The Narrow Road to the Interior* and commended it to me. Hahn uses Murasaki's work as well as Bashō's *The Narrow Road to the Interior* to comment on her own life. The woman who invited these pages into being does not speak here but remains present.

Hahn, Kimiko: *The Narrow Road to the Interior.* New York, W.W. Norton & Co., 2006. My copy of the Bashō is called *The Narrow Road to the Deep North and Other Travel Sketches,* translated by Nobuyuki Yuasa. London, Penguin Books, 1966.

"There's a certain grain of stupidity. . .": Flannery O'Connor

"Actually I have written down my experience . . .": Louise Bogan

"The Gate at Visby, I"

The epigraph is from *A Fool's Errand,* Dermot Healy.

The figure described is an exhibit in Gotlands Fornsal, Gotland's Historical Museum, as are the picture-stones.

Words in italics in that poem quote labels in the museum.

"The Gate at Visby, II"

The exclamation *Sommar! Sommar! Ljuva Sommar!* means *Summer! Summer! Glorious Summer!* and appears on signs all over Visby.

"Sarcophagus"

Sarcophagus: *A kind of stone reputed among the Greeks to have he property of consuming the flesh of dead bodies deposited in it, and consequently used for coffins.*
–OED

Acknowledgements

The language of the dedication is from Donald Platt's "Dirt Angels," in the volume of the same name. Used with kind permission.

*

The author is grateful to the editors of publications who first published these poems, often in a different form.

Barrow Street: "In the Medieval Sculpture Hall"

Chance of a Ghost, Gloria Vando and Philip Miller, Eds., Helicon Nine Editions: "Visit"

Chest: Journal of the American College of Chest Physicians: "A Change of Heart"

Comstock Review: "Oxen, Harnesses," "View with Water and Prepositions"

Diode: "Forgiveness, an Abstract," "Great-Grandmother Comes to Me in a Dream," "Souk, Akko"

Exit Online: "The Tiger in the Driveway"

Earth's Daughters: "The Long Emptying"

laFovea.org: "A Loaf of Bread," "What Takes Us Down"

Negative Capability: "Notes from a Bicycle Trip with Marianne Moore in Rock Springs, Wyoming"

NYCBigCityLit.com: "Winter," "Paul's House" (as "One Day Beside the Delaware"), "(On Not) Believing in an Afterlife"

Persimmontree.org: "The Palace at 4 AM"

Serving House Journal: "At Masada"

Shofar (Purdue University; Special Issue on Jewish Poetry): "Stalheim," "Palaces of Glass and Stone"

The Literary Review: "The Man with the Sword"

The Same: "Interior, Gulf Coast" (as "Bank Building, Gulf Coast"), reprinted in *In the Black / in the Red: Poems of Profit and Loss,* Helicon Nine Editions

✦

The author wishes to express her appreciation to The Baltic Centre for Writers and Translators, Hawthornden Castle International Retreat for Writers, and The Corporation of Yaddo.

Extraordinary appreciation wrapped in admiration to Phil Memmer, Steve Huff, Don Platt.

Heartfelt thanks to the two Georges: George in Saudi and George here.

Warmest appreciation to Carol, Charlotte, Kay, Tom, Chris, Chet and Toni, Sharon, Laure-Anne, Gayle and Joffy, Maria, and Martin. Warm regards and permanent thanks to Don Hall, Molly, Alicia; Michael.

About the Author

Deena Linett lived for many years in northern New Jersey, and is now in Indiana. She has published prize-winning novels and short stories. This is her third collection of poems.

In addition to fellowships to The Baltic Centre for Writers and Translators on Gotland, she has twice been resident at Hawthornden Castle International Retreat for Writers outside Edinburgh, and twice a Yaddo Fellow.

www.deenalinett.org